IS YOUR AMBITION MEANINGFUL?

To help you discover the meaningful ambitions that bring joy to your life and positively impact the world around you.

Dr Mohamed Nismy Rafiudeen, PhD

PUBLICATION DATA
Name: Is Your Ambition Meaningful?
First edition: February 2024
Written and published by Mohamed Nismy Rafiudeen

CONTENTS

ABOUT THE BOOK

You are in the right place if you are determined to make your life meaningful.

This book has been written for you. After seeing and working with hundreds of people, including young people, professionals, entrepreneurs, and academicians, we found that the primary reason for their stagnation is a lack of clarity about their future, i.e., no clear ambition.

This book will help you have a comprehensive view of ambition.

Chapter 1: What's ambition? - We begin by unravelling the concept of ambition and understanding its essence and role in shaping our aspirations and goals.

Chapter 2: What are the Positive and negative impacts of having ambition? - We delve into the dual nature of ambition, examining its positive effects, such as driving us toward success and its negative impacts, such as fostering unhealthy competition.

Chapter 3: How to distinguish genuine ambitions from mere wishes? - We navigate the fine line between genuine ambitions rooted in personal values and fleeting desires influenced by external pressures.

Chapter 4: How to set a meaningful ambition? - We offer practical guidance on setting ambitions aligned with our true selves, values, and strengths, fostering personal fulfilment and growth.

Chapter 5: How to balance personal ambition with a career that's not aligned with ambition? - We address the challenge of reconciling personal ambitions with professional responsibilities that may not fully align with our aspirations.

Chapter 6: Setting meaningful ambition is stepping out of your comfort zone—Finally, we explore the transformative journey of stepping out of our comfort zones to pursue ambitions that lead to profound personal development and self-realisation.

We have provided many examples in each chapter to elaborate on the various ideas.

At the end of each chapter, examples of famous personalities related to the content of the chapter are given. In addition, quizzes are provided to enhance your understanding in terms of comprehension, critical thinking, and application.

Welcome to a journey of self-discovery and personal growth as we delve into the depths of ambition and its profound impact on our lives.

Dr Mohamed Nismy Rafiudeen, PhD
Human Resource Development Strategist

I

WHAT IS AMBITION?

The notion of 'ambition' is deep-seated in our ethos and intensely intertwined into our lives.

From childhood, you hear this word, resonating in the questions asked by elders: "What is your ambition?" While natural in its intent, this question has taught the idea of futuristic thinking in your mind.

You reply to this question based on your hearing and seeing, and your surroundings inspire you.

The influence of peers and the media is mostly very high. The hero, heroines, and sports stars might have become your role models.

When you grow up, the idea of 'ambition' fades. Eventually, you may not have a solid answer: "What is your ambition?"

It's pathetic that many people are unaware of their ambitions or direction in life. Instead, they are besieged by wishful ideas and struggle to overcome their situation.

Most of them lose their way due to the whims of fate and are lost at dead ends.

Though 'ambition' is universal, its meaning has been understood differently. Most people consider mere wishes to be ambitions.

Therefore, this chapter aims to provide a broader understanding of the idea of ambition.

Ambition incorporates a broader range of aspirations, pushing and pulling people to exceed their limitations and contribute to superior ideals.

An individual driven by ambition is not content with short-term achievements but is motivated to bring more significant changes, uplift the communities, or create a legacy of sustainable impacts.

Thus, ambitious people become innovative, creative, and tireless to drive towards excellence. Further, they inspire others to follow in their footsteps.

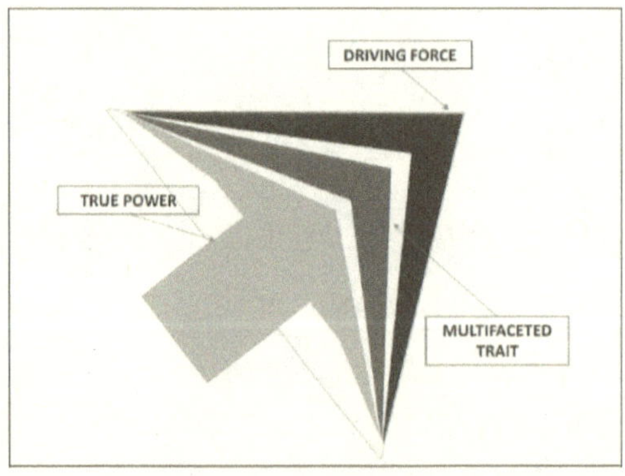

Eventually, they build a unique mindset that helps them see the obstacles as challenges and stepping stones to climb higher and higher. Thus, ambition is a driving force, a multifaceted trait, and a true power that energises individuals to flourish and leave a lifelong impact on their institutions, communities, and the world.

A DRIVING FORCE

Ambition is a driving force. It is the internal drive to reach what one deserves in line with one's potential.

Ambition ignites its owner, provides continuous energy, and makes him feel great, even though toxic people and the environment surround him.

Ambition catalyses growth regardless of the situation and pulls one to reach what one desires or deserves..

a) Imagine you are a high school student who aspires to become an expert in the field that interests you.

   Your family background, financial situation, examinations and competitions among the students may become obstacles for you.

   However, you will overcome with courage to walk towards your ambition.

   You will set high-end milestones, such as securing a place at a prestigious university to study under top-level experts in your field.

   The students around you will witness the force that drives you through all the challenges they see as obstacles.

   Hence, your ambition is evident in all your endeavours, including studies, engaging in additional learning activities, and exploring all the possibilities to enter the best university that will open doors for your future.

b) Consider that you are a young professional who aspires to become a leader in your preferred industry.

   Your ambition will keep you busy. You will invest time and money to advance your career by undertaking challenging projects and continuously improving your essential knowledge and skills.

   Your colleagues will witness your proactive approaches to seeking new opportunities, respecting and learning from experienced people, and connecting with influential professionals.

c) If you are a budding entrepreneur determined to set up your own business, observe yourself and notice that you are driving at your super speed.

   Your ambition to achieve financial freedom will be there in front of you.

   You will connect all the possibilities, challenge all the obstacles on your path, push boundaries, and ultimately realise your ambition of launching a venture.

d) Picture yourself as an individual who is focusing on personal development.

   Your ambition to become physically and mentally healthy is evident in your regular schedule, which includes regular exercise, eating and sleeping habits, and practising spiritual activities. Eventually, you will become your best version.

You notice that your ambition is driving you to become better than yesterday.

Thus, ambition is a driving force if you have set the right ambition. Your ambition becomes your driver. However, if your ambition does not force or activate you, you must review and revise it immediately.

A MULTIFACED TRAIT

When ambition drives you, you will notice some unique traits emerge within you, such as the pursuit of excellence, the willingness to take risks, and the courage to overcome obstacles to your ambition.

You will be persistent, committed to progress, and relentlessly seek growth and advancement.

In addition to these benefits, you will enjoy fantastic experiences such as positive attitudes and behaviours across the different stages and diverse walks of your life.

Whether you are a student aspiring to achieve academic success, a professional striving for career advancement, or an entrepreneur working towards a sustainable business venture, your ambition will bring sustainable positive changes within you.

Your ambition is the benchmark for setting your short-term and long-term goals, including your life goal.

Short-term goals include everything you plan to do in your daily, weekly, and monthly life and long-term goals related to your education, health, profession, relationship, and spiritual aspects. Hence, your ambition is deeply intertwined with every aspect of your life.

Continual improvement will become your daily routine, and you will see the challenges as stepping stones towards your ambition.

The other way around, you are moving through a multifaceted approach towards your ambition.

a) Consider that you are a college student facing various academic obstacles. If you are an ordinary student without ambition, those obstacles are sufficient to give up your studies.

   However, you will demonstrate differently if you are an ambitious person.

   Despite all those obstacles, you will remain determined to excel to become a graduate and make a meaningful impact in your chosen field.

   You will enjoy studying long hours, seeking direction from mentors to address the obstacles, and pursuing an internship in a challenging workplace to experience the theories you learned in your course.

b) Imagine you are an experienced professional in a dynamic industry driven by ambition to advance your career and positively influence your organisation's direction. Your ambition will prompt you to seek leadership opportunities, mentor and coach your junior colleagues, and explore innovative ways to drive the company forward.

Your ambition will push you to attend to various aspects that can help you achieve the desired outcomes.

c) Assume you are a seasoned entrepreneur, having achieved your first milestone of launching your business at a prestigious location.

   Your ambition will not stop there. As an ambitious person who wants to create a long-lasting impact in your preferred industry, you will start to explore all the possibilities and opportunities to explore ways and means to establish yourself in the market.

   You will explore how to attract more customers, seek strategic partnering with suppliers and other businesses that align with your supply chain and develop innovative products or services that have the potential to impact the industry.

d) If you are interested in personal development and have achieved noteworthy milestones in your development journey, you will further focus on elevating your overall well-being.

   Hence, you will set new goals to maintain your physical, mental, and spiritual wellness. Then, you will continue to inspire others to follow you through engaging in philanthropic activities.

Your unyielding ambition will propel you to push the boundaries of your comfort zone, embrace new experiences, and positively impact your community while continuing to evolve and thrive.

Thus, having ambition makes people vibrant and allows them to experience multifaceted changes to become successful.

A TRUE POWER

In pursuing ambition, people encounter various obstacles and setbacks that test and qualify their capability to move from one milestone to another.

While an ordinary person walks on a flat path, an ambitious person climbs over the steps.

While walking the same distance horizontally, the ambitious person moves vertically. He will have the energy to lift his body and climb upward from his ambition.

Your ambition is power. It is the fuel that ignites all your faculties to work synchronously.

Your eyes, ears, and tongue will work more productively than ordinary people.

You will see what others do not see, hear what others do not, and say what others do not speak.

Hence, the people around you will witness high standards in your learning and communication.

The weight of the challenges will showcase the strength of your ambition. In other words, when you overcome every challenge, you will experience the power you gain from your ambition.

When you face adversity, your ambition will boost your confidence and resilience and ignite your brain to generate innovative ways to overcome it and move forward.

a) Imagine you are a graduate student pursuing a doctoral degree in a field known for its rigorous demands and intense competition.

   Despite the obstacles, your ambition to contribute original research to your preferred field will propel you to excel in your coursework, research, and academic contributions to your field.

   Your ambition will fuel your perseverance through spending long hours in the literature review, interviewing subject matter experts, and leading professionals to deliver a contribution that will bring your industry from where it is to where it should be to cater for the present and future demands.

b) As a seasoned executive, you will seek to use your influence to drive positive change within your institution and across your industry. Your ambition will lead you to advocate for diversity and inclusion, sustainability, and ethical business practices to create a lasting impact that transcends your career success.

Your unwavering ambition will propel you to become highly visible in your industry, discover your potential, take leadership roles, and work tirelessly to drive meaningful transformation within your influence.

c) Imagine that you are now an established entrepreneur, having achieved success with multiple ventures; you will expand the scope of your ambition to set your sights on a new endeavour that addresses a pressing global challenge.

   Your ambition will drive you to identify and work with diverse teams, secure investments, get involved with experts, and drive innovation that could improve the lives of people beyond you're the borders you set initially.

   Your ambition will fuel your dedication to realising a global vision that will impact people's lives.

d) As an individual who has overcome significant personal challenges and inspired and guided others facing similar struggles, you will now expand the scope of your ambition to become an advocate, mentor, and motivational speaker.

   You will share your stories and wisdom to empower others to overcome adversity and pursue their dreams.

   Your unshakable ambition will fuel your commitment and determination to make a lifelong impact, empowering individuals to find strength, resilience, and hope in life's challenges.

In conclusion, ambition is a fundamental element of human nature. It is a driving force, multifaceted trait, and power that can transform you from your present status to Superman. Your ambition will boost your value and drive you to impact your surroundings positively. You will dream big. You will become a hard-working person to deliver what you desire. Hence, having ambition will empower you to take on significant challenges like a hero and ultimately leave a legacy.

Thomas Edison

In the late 19th century, a young boy named Thomas Edison had a burning ambition to become an inventor despite facing numerous setbacks and challenges.

He had dyslexia and struggled with traditional education methods, leading his teachers to label him as "addled" or mentally slow. However, Edison's ambition and determination remained unwavering.

At 12, Edison set up a laboratory in the basement of his family's home, where he conducted numerous experiments and tinkered with various inventions.

Despite facing failures and setbacks, he persisted in his pursuit of innovation. 1879, after thousands of failed attempts, Edison finally invented the first commercially practical incandescent light bulb, revolutionising how people lived and worked.

Edison's story highlights the importance of having ambition in the face of adversity. Despite his struggles and setbacks, he remained focused on his goal and continued to pursue his passion for invention.

His ambition led to groundbreaking discoveries and inspired countless others to dream big and never give up on their aspirations. Edison's story is a powerful reminder that anything is possible with ambition, perseverance, and determination.

REFLECTION

Below are quizzes designed to evaluate your grasp of the chapter's content, your aptitude for critical thinking regarding the discussed concepts, and your ability to apply these concepts in real-life scenarios.

Before proceeding to the next chapter, take some time to review these questions.

Doing so will aid in recalling the chapter's key points and assist you in forming your interpretations.

Quiz 1: Comprehension

1. What is the primary message conveyed in the chapter regarding the notion of ambition?
2. According to the chapter, what factors influence an individual's ambition?
3. Explain the significance of ambition in personal and professional development as outlined in the chapter.
4. Describe the role of ambition in overcoming obstacles and achieving goals, as discussed in the chapter.

Quiz 2: Critical Thinking

1. Do you agree that ambition is a driving force for individuals? Why or why not?
2. How does the chapter differentiate between ordinary and ambitious individuals regarding their approach to challenges?
3. Discuss the importance of setting the right ambition, as highlighted in the chapter.

4. Reflect on a personal or observed experience where ambition played a significant role in achieving a goal or overcoming a challenge. How does it relate to the concepts discussed in the chapter?

Quiz 3: Application

1. Choose one of the scenarios described in the chapter (a, b, c, or d) and analyse how ambition is demonstrated in that situation. Provide specific examples.
2. Imagine you are coaching or mentoring a friend who feels lost and lacks direction in life.

   How would you use the concepts of ambition outlined in the chapter to guide and motivate them?
3. Develop a personal development plan incorporating the principles of ambition discussed in the chapter.

   Outline short-term and long-term goals and strategies for overcoming potential obstacles.

Identify an example of an individual driven by ambition. Describe his or her journey, the challenges faced, and the impact of ambition on his or her surroundings.

2

IMPACT OF AMBITION?

In the first chapter, we discussed 'What is ambition?' Ambition is a driving force, multifaceted trait, and power that activates you to perform in your preferred industry.

Ambition inculcates a strong desire and determination to work hard, dedication, and perseverance.

It is an inner power that propels you to maximise and capitalise on your potential. We discussed that ambition could manifest in various areas of life, including personal growth, career development, and social impact.

However, there are two perceptions of ambition: positive and negative.

While some people talk about the positive impacts of ambition on life, others also say there are negative impacts. This chapter explores both perspectives, their importance, potential negative impacts, and how they influence individuals and society.

POSITIVE IMPACTS	NEGATIVE IMPACTS
Motivation and Drive	Burnout and stress
Goal Setting	Tunnel Vision
Personal Growth	Unethical Behaviour
Innovation and Creativity	Relationship Strain
Resilience	Perfectionism
Career Advancement	Health Neglect
Impact and Influence	Impatience
Confidence	Sense of Inadequacy
Satisfaction and Self-efficacy	Risk of Isolation
Meaningful Contribution	Reduced Enjoyment

POSITIVE IMPACTS OF HAVING AMBITION

1. Motivation and Drive:

   Ambition is similar to having an energetic, enthusiastic, and experienced driver to get you where you want to go.

   Even while you are relaxing or sleeping, you will keep moving. Your mind will be some steps ahead of where you are.

   Ambition will keep you motivated and focused all the time. When you are surrounded by fear, your ambition will give you hope. When threats encircle you, your ambition will show you opportunities. When a toxic environment encloses you, your ambition will save you and move forward confidently.

2. Goal Setting:

   Setting goals, such as education, career, wealth, and health, is crucial. Failing to set goals may waste your resources, time, and efforts.

   Furthermore, setting unaligned goals from different perspectives of your life can eventually make you unproductive.

   Having ambition will make it easy to set the right goals. You will be able to set goals with meaningful targets.

3. Personal Growth:

   Some people, including professionals, are trapped in the same status.

   They say they are happy about where and what they are doing. They are living without ambitions.

   However, you will not stay at the same level for two consecutive days if you are ambitious.

   Your ambition will push you beyond your comfort zone and expand your capabilities.

   If you assess your progress regularly, you will witness you continuously developing your knowledge, skills, and abilities. You will experience a thirst for self-improvement and a willingness to embrace challenges that foster growth.

4. Innovation and Creativity:

   Walking towards an ambition enhances innovation and creativity.

   You will seek new solutions, explore novel ideas, and challenge existing norms.

   You will be propelled to think outside the box and explore unconventional approaches. The people around you will witness your curiosity.

5. Resilience:

   Resilience in the face of obstacles and failures is one of the characteristics an ambitious person eventually develops.

   You will explore ways and means to face the challenges and learn to prepare for similar situations in the future.

   Your ambition instils the mental fortitude required to overcome setbacks and failures.

   Hence, you will bounce back from disappointments.

   Further, you will become stronger and stronger in navigating through turbulence, like a competent captain driving his ship during a storm.

6. Career Advancement:

   An ambitious professional will enjoy a successful career that offers career advancement, job satisfaction, and financial stability.

   You will be mentally and physically prepared to take on new responsibilities.

   While your colleagues are happy about their current jobs, you will perform well and be appreciated by your supervisors.

7. Impact and Influence:

   Ambitious individuals impact the people around them. While your ambition drives you, people will follow the trend you create.

   They will benefit from your work and happily support you when you are in trouble.

   When they find that being with or supporting you may bring them happiness and solve their problems, they will make you, their leader.

   Depending on the scope and scale of your ambition, you will reach out and impact people's lives.

8. Confidence and Self-Efficacy:

   An ambitious individual gradually develops confidence and self-efficacy.

You will believe in your abilities and stand up on your feet. Any external factors can not disturb and detract from your ambition because you are not depending on them.

The people around you may misunderstand your confidence as stubbornness. However, when times come, they will be behind you.

9. Satisfaction:

Working towards an ambition gives satisfaction in life. When you achieve the goals you have set in your life, alignment with your ambition will bring you happiness and a sense of fulfilment.

You will experience profound satisfaction, knowing that your hard work has borne fruit.

You will realise how all the difficulties and hard times throughout your journey help you reach your goals safely and will enthusiastically share those experiences with your people.

10. Meaningful Contributions:

Ambitious people contribute to developing a better community organisation.

The community you are witnessing is the result of the ambitious people of the past. Similarly, your contribution will be remembered by future generations.

Hence, having ambition will leave a meaningful legacy and imprint on the world around you and beyond.

NEGATIVE IMPACT OF HAVING AMBITION

When we talk about the positive impact of ambition, there is a notion that criticises its adverse effects on people's lives.

The negative impacts arise due to unchecked ambitions, which can have unfavourable effects on various aspects of one's life.

In this section, we aim to provide insight into the importance of genuine ambition in helping you enjoy a balanced and fulfilling life.

1. Burnout and Stress:

   Ambitious people often feel trapped, leading to burnout and chronic stress.

   If the ambition they are striving for is not genuine, they will become exhausted.

   Although their hard work may help them achieve what they want, their misalignment with their may lead them to unfulfillment.

   Furthermore, lack of rest and relentless pursuit may cause physical and mental health issues.

2. Tunnel Vision:

   Without proper guidance, some ambitious individuals may develop 'tunnel vision'.

Eventually, they will sacrifice other essential aspects of their lives, such as health and well-being.

Further, their determination may severely affect the people around them.

3. Unethical Behaviour:

   When ambitious individuals are intensely driven by their ambitions, they may behave unethically and attempt to achieve their goals at any cost, compromising integrity and moral values.

   Strangely, they do not realise the trouble they cause the people around them.

4. Relationship Strain:

   Excessive focus on ambition can damage relationships with others.

   Youths will be distant from their parents, and professionals will become busy and away from spouses and children.

   Eventually, their lives will become imbalanced, leading to feelings of neglect, isolation, and discord within their relationships.

5. Perfectionism:

   Ambition can lead to perfectionism. If people set unrealistic ambitions, they will not be happy until they achieve what they deserve.

The relentless pursuit of excellence may result in constant inadequacy, leading to anxiety and discontent.

6. Health Neglect:

   Overwhelming ambition might lead to a loss of attention to self-care.

   They may neglect healthy eating and sufficient sleep. They will not eat until they are satisfied with their work.

   They will work until midnight, sometimes until dawn. Eventually, they will become physically weak and end up with several health issues.

7. Impatience:

   Impatience might be another consequence of excessive ambition.

   Impatient people become frustrated when they do not achieve results, which can lead to adverse outcomes.

   Team members will be badly affected, especially when working in a team, and their reputation will gradually be lost.

8. Sense of Inadequacy:

   If the ambition is not genuine and reasonable, it might cause a perpetual sense of inadequacy.

   The effort required for unrealistic ambition compared to genuine ambition is very high and stressful.

Hence, people who are working on unreasonable ambition can feel unsatisfied.

Eventually, effects such as a chronic sense of dissatisfaction and a sense of inadequacy might occur.

9. Risk of Isolation:

   People who overemphasise their ambition might end up in isolation.

   They will avoid disturbance from friends and family, think deeply, and explore solutions to problems.

   In the beginning, they will justify that isolation. However, their loved ones are used to their behaviours and gradually forget them.

10. Reduced Enjoyment:

    Ambitious people celebrate only when they achieve milestones.

    The rest of the time, they are serious about their work and avoid social interactions.

    The relentless focus on ambition should not overshadow the pleasures of the process itself. They fail to realise the nature of life, and they may regret it later in life.

In conclusion, having ambition does not cause negative impacts. Instead, not choosing genuine ambition and lack of clarity in life may negatively impact a person's life. This is like using a beneficial tool such as a knife. When you don't know how to use it, you will end up in chaos. Therefore, having ambition is always beneficial. However, you must be careful when you set your ambition to make it genuine. Consequently, knowing how to distinguish genuine ambition from mere wishes is essential. Because the negative impacts, as discussed above, arise from having mere wishes as ambitions. The next chapter will help you to understand the differences between genuine ambition and mere wishes.

Albert Einstein

In the late 19th century, a young man named Albert Einstein had a deep passion for learning and a natural curiosity about the world. However, despite his intellectual gifts, Einstein struggled in traditional educational settings due to his rebellious nature and unconventional approach to learning. Einstein's lack of clear ambition initially hindered his academic career. He dropped out of high school in Germany and struggled to find employment, working odd jobs and tutoring students to make ends meet. Einstein's early career was uncertain and frustrating without a clear direction or ambition.

However, Einstein's life dramatically turned when he discovered his passion for theoretical physics and pursued ambitious scientific inquiries. Despite facing numerous setbacks and rejections, Einstein remained determined to unravel the mysteries of the universe through his groundbreaking theories of relativity and quantum mechanics.

Eventually, Einstein's ambition and relentless pursuit of knowledge propelled him to international fame and acclaim. His theories revolutionised our understanding of space, time, and the nature of reality, earning him the Nobel Prize in Physics in 1921 and cementing his legacy as one of the most outstanding scientists ever.

Einstein's story powerfully reminds us of the importance of clear ambition in education and career success. Despite his early struggles and lack of direction, Einstein's passion for learning and ambition to unlock the universe's secrets ultimately led him to greatness. His journey inspires us to pursue our passions with clarity and determination, knowing that ambition is the key to unlocking our full potential.

REFLECTION

Here are some quizzes crafted to gauge your understanding of the chapter's content, your ability to think critically about the concepts discussed, and your capacity to apply these concepts in real-life situations.

Before you move on to the next chapter, review these questions.

This will help reinforce the chapter's key points and enable you to develop your insights.

Quiz 1: Comprehension

1. What are the three main attributes of ambition discussed in the chapter?
2. List three positive impacts of having ambition as outlined in the chapter.
3. Name three negative impacts of unchecked ambition according to the chapter.
4. How does the chapter conclude regarding the relationship between ambition and its potential negative impacts?

Quiz 2: Critical Thinking

1. Do you agree with the statement that having ambition is always beneficial? Why or why not?

   Provide examples to support your argument.
2. Discuss the concept of "genuine ambition" versus "mere wishes" as presented in the chapter.

   Why is it important to differentiate between the two?
3. Reflect on a personal or observed experience where ambition led to positive and negative outcomes.

How could a better understanding of ambition have altered the outcome?

4. Analyse the potential consequences of perfectionism stemming from ambition.

   How might this impact an individual's mental health and overall well-being?

Quiz 3: Application

1. Choose one positive and negative impact of ambition discussed in the chapter.

   Provide a real-life example of each and discuss how they manifest in the individual's life.

2. Develop a plan to help someone struggling with the negative impacts of ambition outlined in the chapter.

   Include strategies for identifying and addressing unhealthy ambition.

3. Imagine you are advising a young professional on how to harness the positive aspects of ambition while mitigating the negative impacts.

   Provide actionable steps they can take to achieve this balance.

Identify a historical figure or contemporary leader known for their ambition. Discuss how their ambition influenced positive and negative outcomes in their lives and society.

3

MERE WISHES

As discussed in previous chapters, 'ambition' is a force and power that drives an individual to become a meaningful person and contribute to humanity.

People set ambitions for various areas of their lives, such as academic, career, personal, and community development.

When we examine people's ambitions closely, it becomes clear that many have set their ambitions influenced by mere wishes owned by themselves or by external forces, such as peers, parents, teachers, colleagues, media representations, and community expectations.

This chapter will discuss wishful ambitions influenced by others and their impact.

Further, we will discuss the importance of basing on the innate potential to discover the ambition that will provide fulfilment and the sustainable power to lead life meaningfully.

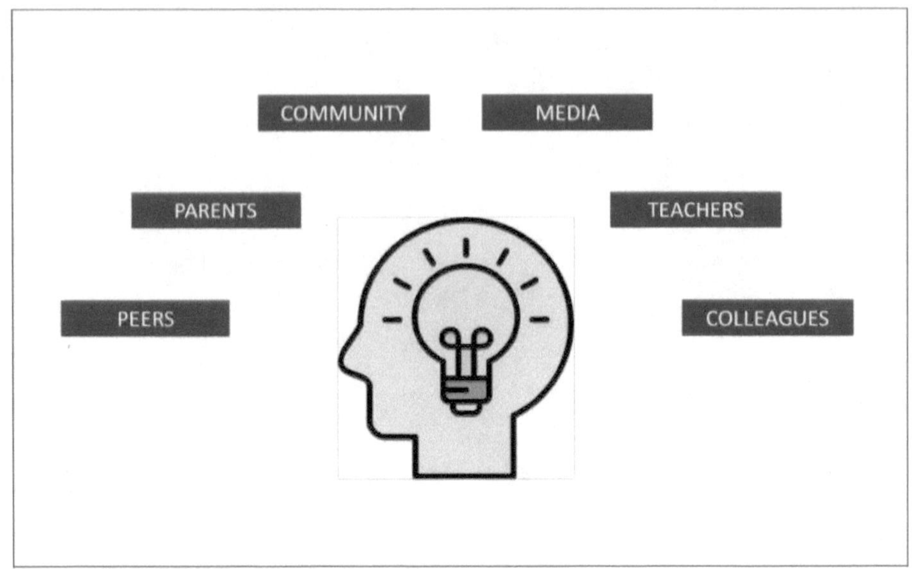

PEER INFLUENCE

Peer influence from childhood is a significant aspect that significantly shapes one's life, especially ambition.

Most people's childhood and teenage years are full of joy and excitement with friends.

They explore and decide everything in their narrow world. Gradually, they shape their worldview, react, and gain hands-on experiences.

Accordingly, the thoughts and feelings they gain gradually construct their belief system and propel them to develop life ambitions. Those ambitions seem very superficial. However, some of them shape their life accordingly.

For instance, consider a scenario where a group of friends is intensely interested in pursuing medical careers due to societal prestige and financial stability. Despite having a potential for art, individuals may feel compelled to conform to their peers' ambitions and overlook their artistic potential.

Similarly, students may choose certain subjects to stay in the same classroom with their friends in Academic settings. For example, a student may select biology despite having a natural aptitude for literature.

These examples illustrate how peer pressure can steer individuals away from their true potential.

Therefore, it is essential to emphasise the need to cultivate independence in discovering their ambitions by encouraging them to explore their potential autonomously.

INFLUENCE OF PARENTS

Parents play a significant role in influencing their children to set ambitions.

This is a normal and highly accepted practice in society from the perspective of 'children are not capable of making right decisions about their future'.

Parents always think suitable for their children, which is true of teachers.

For instance, a parent may encourage their child to become an Engineer because of its prestige by overlooking their child's potential. However, their child might be able to become a musician or sportsperson.

In this case, parents inject their preferences into the child's mind with good intentions.

However, they don't know that they are opening a door for their child to face many unwelcome challenges throughout life.

INFLUENCE OF TEACHERS

Teachers play a significant role in influencing their children to set ambitions.

Teachers may emphasise certain academic subjects or career paths based on their measures of success rather than helping the students discover their genuine ambition.

These pressures from parents and teachers may form unauthentic ambitions, leading individuals to pursue things that are unaligned with their aspirations.

However, parents and teachers are responsible for observing children's potential and helping them build their futures.

Programs like "Lead your child!" and "Lead your student!" are becoming important for parents and teachers to know their parenting and teaching responsibilities, which are not discussed or taught anywhere else. [1]

INFLENCE OF COLLEGUES

In the professional world, people develop their career dreams

---

[1] For information about these programs, see this book's last page.

based on what they see in their working environment.

When professionals enter the job market, they are exceptionally inspired by their supervisors, seniors, or colleagues to draft their career ambitions of getting higher positions.

For instance, a professional may quickly climb the hierarchical ladder by prioritising financial gain, regardless of his potential and personal values.

COMMUNITY INFLUENCE

Another scenario is the social pressure that makes professionals choose their career ambitions.

Consider the case of a young professional who, despite having a potential for environmental conservation, feels compelled to pursue a career in finance due to societal pressures regarding the prestige and financial rewards associated with the field.

Similarly, cultural norms within certain communities may strongly emphasise specific career paths rather than pursuing their authentic aspirations.

For instance, in some cultures, individuals may have a prevailing expectation to pursue careers in medicine, law, or engineering, regardless of their potential.

Academically brilliant students with excellent teaching skills might be prompted to become doctors or engineers. Eventually, our schools will have a group of teachers who are academically poor. In brief, these external forces lead to unfulfillment and dissonance.

It's an individual responsibility to follow the right criteria, especially long-term decisions and ambitions. Hence, creating self-awareness is crucial for young professionals.

INFLUENCE OF MEDIA

In the contemporary world, the media plays an influential role in shaping individuals' ambitions.

Current media brings the entire world between the fingers. People can choose what they want to see and hear by one touch.

Hence, their minds intake a vast amount of information. While more information has many advantages, decision-making becomes highly complicated, especially when discovering ambitions.

With the presence of celebrity culture and the rise of social media influencers, people are constantly flooded with curated narratives that mould their understanding of achievement.

For example, platforms like Instagram and TikTok often showcase seemingly glamorous lifestyles, reinforcing that success is synonymous with wealth, fame, and material possessions.

This can create unrealistic expectations and fuel a desire for instant pleasure, leading individuals to prioritise superficial markers of success over more meaningful pursuits.

Moreover, this can eventually contribute to feelings of inadequacy and self-doubt as people measure their achievements against seemingly flawless depictions in the media.

Hence, educating students and youth on healthy media consumption is essential to helping them form ambitions.

Adopting a mindful approach to media consumption, such as seeing the media as a supporting agency rather than a primary source for decision-making, can immensely assist individuals and protect them from the negative impact of the media.

MISCONCEPTION OF AMBITION

There is a widespread misunderstanding that 'ambition is a job title'.

For example, an individual says, 'I want to become a 'science teacher'. Another person says, 'I want to teach science'. Which person has ambition out of these two?

The first person aspires to get a title (teacher) and may not teach science if he fails to become a teacher.

However, the second person aspires to teach science, whether or not he gets the title 'teacher'.

Thus, ambition is about a work or role you aspire to perform in the future rather than a job title.

If an individual says, "I want to become a medical doctor, an engineer, or a politician," you must ask them why they want to do so. You must make them think about values. Because Job titles are embedded with 'money'.

Another misunderstanding about ambition exists among people

across society: ambition is anything they have to achieve in the future, which will motivate them to act upon it.

This narrow understanding leads people to chase after something that does not reflect what they deserve, ultimately resulting in discord and dissatisfaction, even if they attain external signs of success.

For instance, someone may set out to climb the corporate ladder or accumulate wealth without considering whether these pursuits genuinely resonate with their potential and values.

As a result, they may achieve their goals after so many efforts and sacrifices. However, they will say those achievements do not bring happiness and a sense of fulfilment.

When individuals take mere wishes as their ambitions, they often face negative consequences. These can include feeling dissatisfied, experiencing burnout, and struggling to maintain motivation.

Furthermore, choosing career paths ultimately leaves one feeling disengaged in career or life.

When someone sets a 'Genuine Ambition', they will not face these adverse outcomes but lead a more fulfilling life.

This concept of 'Genuine Ambition' underscores certain principles behind setting ambitions instead of being attracted to or influenced by external factors, such as peers, parents, teachers, colleagues, and the community, as discussed in this chapter.

Drawing upon insights from this chapter, we distinguished genuine ambitions from mere wishes. External pressures or momentary desires do not influence genuine Ambitions and often influence mere wishes.

Genuine Ambition is a complex phenomenon built upon potential. The next chapter will help you understand 'Genuine Ambition' and how to discover it.

Steve Jobs

During his early years, Steve Jobs dropped out of college and struggled to find his direction in life. He dabbled in various pursuits, including meditation retreats and travelling to India for spiritual enlightenment. Despite his interest in technology and electronics, Jobs lacked a clear ambition and drifted between jobs aimlessly.

However, everything changed for Jobs when he co-founded Apple Inc. with Steve Wozniak in 1976. Inspired by his vision of creating user-friendly personal computers, Jobs poured his energy and ambition into building Apple into a revolutionary technology company.

Jobs' newfound ambition and passion for innovation fuelled Apple's success and solidified his reputation as a visionary leader. Despite facing setbacks, including being ousted from Apple in the 1980s, Jobs remained resilient and pursued his ambitious vision.

Upon returning to Apple in the late 1990s, Jobs revitalised the company, leading it to become one of the world's most valuable and influential technology companies. His relentless pursuit of excellence and commitment to meaningful innovation propelled Apple to unprecedented success.

Job's story powerfully reminds us of the transformative power of meaningful ambition. Once Jobs found his passion and purpose, he channelled his energy and creativity into building a company that would change the world. His journey inspires us to discover and pursue our ambitions with dedication and perseverance, knowing that meaningful ambition can lead to extraordinary success.

REFLECTION

Here are some quizzes designed to evaluate your understanding of the chapter's content, your critical thinking skills regarding the concepts discussed, and your ability to apply these concepts in real-life situations.

Before proceeding to the next chapter, please take a moment to review these questions.

This will help solidify the chapter's key points and empower you to develop your own insights.

1. **Quiz 1: Comprehension**

    1. Provide examples of how peer influence can shape individuals' ambitions.
    2. Discuss the role of parents and teachers in influencing children's ambitions, highlighting potential challenges.
    3. How does the media shape individuals' ambitions in the contemporary world?
    4. Differentiate between genuine ambition and mere wishes, as outlined in the chapter.

Quiz 2: Critical Thinking

1. Reflect on the statement, "Ambition is a force and power that drives an individual to become a meaningful person and contribute to humanity."

   Do you agree or disagree? Provide reasons for your answer.
2. Analyse the potential consequences of individuals pursuing ambitions influenced by external pressures rather than their innate potential and values.
3. Discuss the significance of creating self-awareness in discovering genuine ambitions, especially in the professional world.

4. Reflect on the misunderstanding that "ambition is a job title" discussed in the chapter.

   How can educators help individuals redefine their ambitions beyond job titles?

Quiz 3: Application

1. Choose one example of how peer influence shapes ambitions and discuss strategies to encourage individuals to explore their potential autonomously.
2. Develop a plan to educate students or young professionals on healthy media consumption practices to mitigate the negative impact of media influence on ambition formation.
3. Imagine you are coaching a student torn between pursuing a career influenced by societal pressures and following their genuine ambition.

   How would you guide them in making this decision?

Identify a real-life scenario where someone pursued a career path influenced by external pressures rather than their genuine ambition. Discuss the consequences they faced and what they could have done differently.

4

GENUINE AMBITION

Having a genuine ambition means you have discovered your FUTURE.

Individuals with genuine ambition and those lured by mere wishes live in two worlds. While genuine ambitions contribute to humanity's development, others damage it.

A genuine ambition is a powerful guiding light that helps the holder of the light, and the people around will benefit.

Genuine ambitions cultivate the sense of purpose, motivation, and direction that drive them to create and experience miracles in their personal, professional, and social lives.

This chapter discusses the critical steps to discovering genuine ambition. We provide a step-by-step procedure for discovering your Genuine Ambition. The following simple diagram illustrates the steps.

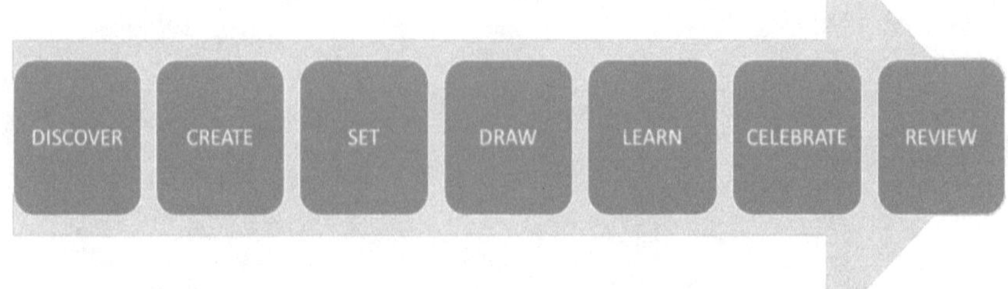

STEP – 1: DISCOVER YOURSELF

Discovering your genuine ambition starts with finding yourself. It is about engaging in deep self-reflection, which includes being aware of the values and potential you bring from birth.

This involves exploring your natural interests, strengths, and aspirations in your life, both personally and professionally. Consider the following questions to guide your self-reflection:

1. What core values govern your life in normal and abnormal situations?

2. What are the most significant interests in your life that you would like to know about and contribute to?

3. What are the strengths do you see within you?

4. What are your long-term aspirations in various areas of your life, such as career, relationships, personal development, and contribution to society?

5. What impact do you want to have on the world?

The answers you come up with for the above questions will help you to understand "Who are you?". How much you know about yourself is crucial to understanding what kind of person you can be in the future.

Hence, you should engage in deep self-examination to identify yourself.

Self-assessments and mindfulness practices can aid in uncovering one's natural potential and guiding the formulation of genuine ambitions.

While some people can perform the self-reflection independently, many require support from mentors and coaches.[2]

> **Example**: Sarah, a marketing professional from a rural village, felt dissatisfied about her work, even though she was earning an excellent salary from her current job. That dissatisfaction bothered her day and night. While she was aware of her leadership skills, she was unclear about what to do and how to do it.
>
> Sara approached an executive coach and engaged in self-reflection to clarify her ambitions.
>
> Finally, she realised she was deeply interested in environmental conservation rather than marketing something else.

---

[2] For information about these programs, see this book's last page.

STEP – 2: CREATE YOUR VISION

Once you understand 'who you are?', the next step is to consider the impact you are expected to create in your preferred industry.

Translating these into a compelling vision—the ultimate change you want to experience in the long run is essential.

Your vision should explain the outcome you are striving for and serve as a source of inspiration and motivation.

> **Example**: Based on her reflections, Sarah envisions a future where every individual in the community will live an environmentally friendly life so that the coming generations will enjoy a healthy life.
>
> Hence, Sara discovered her genuine ambition to preserve the environment to ensure a healthy life for the present and future generations.

STEP - 3: SET YOUR GOALS

Having a beautiful ambition is not enough. It is important to set milestones as well.

Since you know what you intend to deliver in the long run, you must set goals to achieve your ambition step by step.

It's essential to think from multiple perspectives, which will help you achieve your ambition and set goals from each perspective.

The perspectives provide the strategic direction to set, revise, and re-establish goals.

Example: Sarah sets specific goals with the help of her coach from five perspectives: personal education, legal, organisation, finance, and community. She set goals to complete a certification program in environmental sustainability within the next year, get approval from government authorities within the next six months, set up a non-profit organisation within the next year, secure a grant for her initial project within the next year, and promote her vision and attract community support within the next six months.

STEP – 4: DRAW YOUR PLAN

Once you have set the goals, creating an action plan that outlines the steps and strategies is essential.

It is about breaking down the goals into actionable tasks, assigning resources, and creating a timeline for execution.

Resources can be tangible or intangible, including finance, goodwill, network, and everything required to execute the planned tasks.

Example: Sarah has drafted an action plan that includes significant tasks.

Such as enrolling in a relevant certification program, networking with professionals in the sustainability field, renting an office, researching potential grant opportunities, and building a solid case for her project proposal.

In this case, her coach helped her prioritise the tasks

according to their importance and the availability of resources.

Furthermore, each perspective allowed her to see her ambition comprehensively.

STEP – 5: LEARN AND GROW

As discussed in the previous chapters, genuine ambition creates a continuing learning and development mindset.

Hence, it is important to look for opportunities for personal and professional development, sharpen existing skills, seek advanced knowledge, and be flexible for meaningful changes.

Working on a scheme for many years will not make people experts. They must have a plan to upgrade themselves to become experts.

Example: Sarah allocated in her action plan to actively participate in workshops, seminars, conferences and networking events related to sustainability, continuously expanding her knowledge and building relationships within the environmental community.

STEP – 6: CELEBRATE YOUR ACHIEVEMENTS

As you make progress towards your ambitions, take the time to acknowledge and celebrate your milestones and achievements.

This act will help you to keep yourself, your team, and the people in your network motivated.

Recognising your progress can boost your motivation, morale, and sense of accomplishment, fuelling your continued pursuit of your ambitions.

> **Example**: Sarah celebrates each milestone in her journey, such as completing her certification program, securing her first partnership, and receiving positive feedback on her project proposal from her stakeholders, including her family. Hence, she ensures positive momentum around her, which helps her continue with confidence and determination.

STEP – 7: REVIEW AND ADJUST

Discovering genuine ambition at the first step is not always easy. It depends on how much you are aware of yourself.

Hence, without waiting to set a perfect ambition, you need to work on what you set along with your coach.

While progressing, you can observe yourself and adjust your ambition until it aligns perfectly with your potential and values.

Furthermore, periodically reviewing and improving the goals, objectives, and targets must ensure they align with your evolving values, aspirations, and circumstances.

> **Example**: After a year of pursuing her ambitions, Sarah reassesses her ambition and ensures that she is moving in the right direction. She observes that she is experiencing true happiness compared to her previous job. She reviews her goals and makes adjustments based on her

experiences, changes in the environmental sector, and shifts in her priorities.

In conclusion, discovering your genuine ambition is a deliberate and empowering process that involves self-discovery, creating a vision, setting goals, planning, and ongoing adaptation. Following these steps and pursuing your ambitions can cultivate a sense of purpose, motivation, and direction to drive you towards impactful outcomes. Aligning ambition with innate potential is a transformative exercise that can lead to profound personal development and fulfilment.

Elon Musk

In the early 2000s, a young entrepreneur named Elon Musk had a bold ambition to revolutionise how people travelled on Earth and beyond. Despite facing scepticism and doubt from many quarters, Musk was determined to pursue his vision of making space travel accessible to the masses and reducing humanity's dependence on fossil fuels.

In 2002, Musk founded SpaceX with the ambitious goal of making space exploration more affordable and sustainable. He poured his fortune into the company, facing numerous setbacks and near-bankruptcy. However, Musk's unwavering ambition and relentless pursuit of his vision drove SpaceX to achieve remarkable milestones, including becoming the first privately funded company to launch a spacecraft into orbit and successfully land reusable rockets.

Meanwhile, Musk founded Tesla to accelerate the world's transition to sustainable energy. Despite facing scepticism from the automotive industry, Musk's ambition drove Tesla to become a leader in electric vehicles, with innovations such as the Model S and Model 3 capturing the public's imagination and transforming the automotive landscape.

Today, SpaceX is revolutionising space travel with its ambitious plans for Mars colonisation and satellite internet, while Tesla continues to push the boundaries of electric vehicle technology. Musk's story serves as a testament to the power of ambition in driving innovation and pushing the boundaries of what is possible. His relentless pursuit of his vision has transformed industries and inspired countless entrepreneurs to dream big.

REFLECTION

Here are some quizzes tailored to assess your comprehension of the chapter's content, your critical thinking skills regarding the discussed concepts, and your ability to apply these concepts in real-life scenarios.

Before moving on to the next chapter, please take a moment to review these questions. Doing so will reinforce the chapter's key points and enable you to develop your insights.

Quiz 1: Comprehension Questions:

1. According to the chapter, what is the significance of self-reflection in discovering genuine ambition?
2. Explain the concept of creating a vision in the context of discovering genuine ambition. Why is it important?
3. How does continuous learning and growth contribute to pursuing genuine ambition, as discussed in the chapter?
4. Why is celebrating achievements considered an important step in discovering genuine ambition?

Quiz 2: Critical Thinking Questions:

1. Reflect on the role of mentors or coaches in assisting individuals in discovering their genuine ambition.

   How can their guidance impact the outcome?

2. Consider the example of Sarah provided in the chapter.

   What challenges might she face in pursuing her genuine ambition, and how can she overcome them?

3. Discuss the consequences of not aligning one's ambition with innate potential and values.

   Provide examples to support your answer.

4. Evaluate the role of continuous learning and growth in maintaining momentum and adaptability in pursuing genuine ambition.

   How can individuals ensure they remain committed to this aspect?

Quiz 3: Application Questions:

1. Imagine you are coaching a student struggling to identify their genuine ambition.

   How would you guide them through the process of self-reflection and goal-setting?

2. Develop a vision statement for a hypothetical individual who has discovered their genuine ambition in the field of education.

   What outcomes would they strive to achieve?

3. Reflect on your own experiences or observations regarding pursuing genuine ambition.

   How has aligning ambition with innate potential led to positive outcomes in your life or others?

Discuss the importance of resilience and adaptability in discovering genuine ambition. Provide examples of how individuals can navigate challenges and setbacks along the way.

5

BALANCING LIFE

When personal ambition and career are seamlessly aligned, individuals experience deep satisfaction and motivation in their professional pursuits.

They enjoy their work, as it allows them to express their potential.

However, having a career that aligns with ambition is an ideal situation.

Those fortunate to have such a career are rare, and they are always happy to perform beyond their limits.

They are innovative and creative and become stars in their organisations.

Yet, people with unaligned ambitions and careers face challenging times. They also become unproductive in their workplace and eventually are criticised by their colleagues and others.

Hence, balancing personal ambition with a career that may not be entirely aligned can be challenging and cause a sense of dissonance.

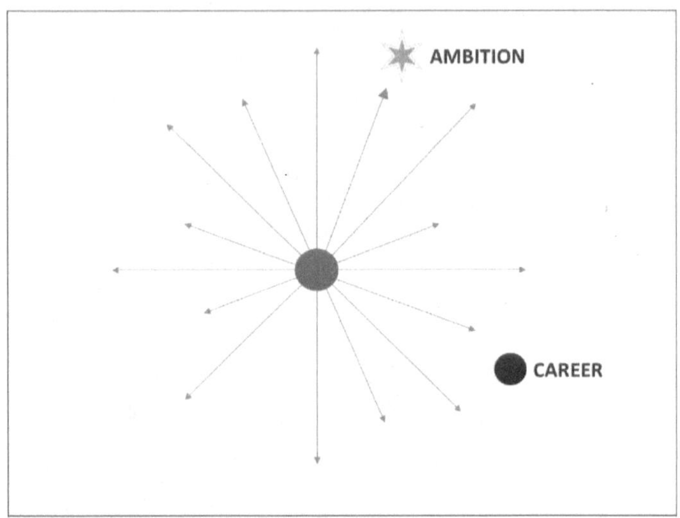

It requires careful consideration and a willingness to explore alternative avenues for personal growth while fulfilling work responsibilities.

How do we handle this situation effectively?

Before exploring the strategies for balancing personal ambition and an unaligned career, it is crucial to recognise the nature of personal ambition and career alignment.

Personal ambition refers to an individual's innate desire to achieve specific goals, fulfil their potential, and make a meaningful impact on their lives and the lives of others.

This can encompass aspirations in various spheres, such as

personal growth, creative endeavours, philanthropy, entrepreneurship, or other pursuits that bring a sense of purpose.

On the other hand, career alignment pertains to the degree to which an individual's profession or job aligns with their values, interests, and long-term goals.

STRATEGIES OF BALANCING

This chapter will discuss balancing unaligned ambition and career and provide examples to illustrate how individuals can navigate this complex scenario.

CLARIFY PERSONAL AMBITIONS

The first step in balancing personal ambition with an unaligned career is to clarify your ambition and take control of your career trajectory.

This involves a powerful self-examination to identify the core areas of natural interest, such as artistic pursuits, community education, or contributing to a specific cause.

Additionally, you should assess your fundamental values, understanding what aspects guide you in life and how these can be integrated into your professional and personal endeavours.

This process empowers you to align your career with your ambitions and values, even if they may not be fully aligned.

Example: Susan, a marketing professional, has always been interested in community education. However, her current career in the fast-paced consumer goods industry does not directly align with these values, leaving her feeling unfulfilled. To balance her ambition with her career, Susan clarifies her ambitions and values. She identifies her strong desire to positively impact the community and live in alignment with her values.

PURSUE PERSONAL DEVELOPMENT OUTSIDE OF WORK

Even if your primary career does not fully align with your ambitions, you can take action and pursue personal development activities outside of your professional responsibilities.

This can involve dedicating time to hobbies, enrolling in courses or workshops related to your interests, volunteering for causes close to your heart, or engaging in creative endeavours that reflect your ambition.

By doing so, you not only enhance your skills and knowledge but also bring a sense of fulfilment and purpose to your life.

This can significantly contribute to your overall happiness and satisfaction, even if your career is not currently aligned with your ambitions.

Example: Hameed, a software engineer, is naturally interested in art and design but finds that his current role as a cashier in a hypermarket leaves little room for creative expression. To balance his ambition with his career, Hameed enrolled in evening art classes and participated in community mural projects outside his work. These activities allow him to channel his creative energy and provide a sense of fulfilment that complements his professional pursuits. Hameed felt that the energy he gained through this strategy helped him perform well in his job compared to previous months.

SEEK OPPORTUNITIES FOR ALIGNMENT OR TRANSITION

When your current career does not align with your ambition, you may seek opportunities within the same organisation or industry that align better.

Additionally, you can consider transitioning to a new career path or industry that more closely aligns with your ambition.

Example: Siva, a finance professional, is interested in social entrepreneurship. Although his current role in a traditional financial firm does not fully align with his desire to drive positive social change through finance, he sought opportunities for alignment or transition. Siva proactively explores roles in impact-driven investment firms and allocates time to network with professionals in the social entrepreneurship space. After careful consideration, he deliberately transitions to a career that allows him to merge his ambition with his professional endeavours.

In conclusion, balancing personal ambition and an unaligned career requires deliberate planning, self-examination, and the courage to pursue personal growth outside one's primary professional responsibilities. By clarifying personal ambitions, pursuing personal development outside of work, and seeking opportunities for alignment or transition, individuals can reconcile the dichotomy between their ambitions and current professional circumstances. Through these strategic steps, you can cultivate a sense of purpose and harmony, ultimately shaping a more holistic and satisfying life journey. Setting ambitious goals often involves venturing beyond your comfort zone, embracing challenges, and persevering through obstacles. But the journey towards realising your ambitions can be enriching in terms of personal growth and contribution to the world around you. The next chapter sheds some insights on this subject of 'ambition and comfort zone'.

J.K. Rowling

J.K. Rowling, the author of the Harry Potter series. Before finding success as a writer, Rowling faced numerous challenges and setbacks in her life. She struggled with depression, went through a difficult divorce, and was a single mother living on welfare benefits. During this time, Rowling felt like a failure and lacked clear ambition for her future. However, she had always been passionate about writing and harboured a deep desire to become a published author. Despite the odds stacked against her, Rowling persevered in pursuing her dream. In 1990, while on a delayed train from Manchester to London, the idea for Harry Potter suddenly came to Rowling. Over the next seven years, she meticulously plotted out the story and characters while balancing the demands of single parenthood and financial hardship.

Rowling faced rejection after rejection from publishers who doubted the commercial viability of her manuscript. However, she refused to give up on her ambition and continued to revise and refine her work. Finally, in 1997, Rowling's perseverance paid off when Bloomsbury Publishing agreed to publish the first Harry Potter book, "Harry Potter and the Philosopher's Stone" (known as "Harry Potter and the Sorcerer's Stone" in the United States). The book was an instant success, captivating readers of all ages and launching Rowling to literary superstardom.

Rowling's journey from struggling single mother to bestselling author is a testament to the transformative power of ambition. Despite facing adversity and uncertainty, she remained steadfast in her determination to become a writer. Rowling's story inspires us to pursue our passions with resilience and determination.

REFLECTION

Here are some quizzes crafted to evaluate your comprehension of the chapter's content, your critical thinking skills regarding the discussed concepts, and your ability to apply these concepts in real-life situations.

Before proceeding to the next chapter, take a moment to review these questions. Doing so will reinforce the chapter's key points and empower you to develop your insights further.

Quiz 1: Personal Ambitions Clarification

- Reflect on your ambitions. What are the core areas of natural interest that drive you?

  How do these align with your current career or professional trajectory?

Quiz 2: Pursuing Personal Development Outside of Work

- Evaluate your current engagement in personal development activities outside your professional responsibilities.

  Can you dedicate more time to hobbies, courses, or creative pursuits?

Quiz 3: Seeking Opportunities for Alignment or Transition

- Assess your current career path and industry. Do you feel that your ambitions are sufficiently aligned with your professional trajectory?

  If not, what opportunities for alignment or transition can you explore?

Quiz 4: Deliberate Planning and Self-Examination

- Reflect on the overall process of balancing personal ambition and an unaligned career.

  How important is deliberate planning and self-examination in this process?

- Consider the strategies discussed in the chapter. Which strategy resonates with you the most, and why?

  How do you plan to implement this strategy in your life and career?

Quiz 5: Cultivating a Sense of Purpose and Harmony

- Reflect on the ultimate goal of balancing personal ambition and career alignment: cultivating a sense of purpose and harmony in life.

  How do you envision achieving this balance in your own life?

Think about the long-term impact of aligning personal ambitions with your career trajectory. How will this alignment contribute to your happiness, satisfaction, and fulfilment?.

6

COMFORT ZONE

Although humans have been created with the nature of living the purpose, the world we are living in has confused them with multiple options.

Therefore, most people are happy to live without direction; instead, they are proud to be unfocused.

This unorganised lifestyle has created an unproductive mindset, and they are prompted to think it is uncomfortable to focus on one direction.

There is another scenario of fear of doing something besides the current job. When they are used to all the pros and cons of their current job and are paid well, their unproductive mind will tell them not to risk stepping into something unfamiliar and all the potential negative consequences.

Hence, setting an ambition means stepping out of your comfort zone.

It is about challenging yourself to embrace new opportunities beyond familiar boundaries.

Therefore, let's discuss in this chapter how you can confidently and successfully carry forward your ambition.

First, you need to comprehend and convince yourself of the importance of living for your genuine ambition.

Indeed, as discussed in previous chapters and hereafter, living with genuine ambition will be immensely rewarding.

In brief, when you dare to step into your ambitious life out of your comfort zone, you are open to a world of possibilities and new experiences.

For example, imagine you have always been interested in painting but have never had opportunities or dared to pick up a brush for various reasons. By pushing yourself to enrol in an art class or engaging with like-minded individuals and exploring your artistic skills, you gain new skills and a deeper understanding of your potential.

Similarly, consider that you have decided to switch careers and pursue a field unrelated to your professional qualifications and previous work experience. While this may initially seem daunting, each challenge you face provides an opportunity for learning and growth, ultimately expanding your horizons and capabilities in ways you never thought possible. Every step beyond the confines of familiarity is a stepping stone towards personal evolution and self-discovery.

Having a genuine ambition makes you resilient and adaptable to uncertain situations.

For instance, imagine you decide to start your own business in an industry where you're naturally interested but have limited experience. Along the way, you might encounter numerous setbacks, such as financial difficulties or unexpected market changes. However, each setback becomes an opportunity for you to learn, adapt, and grow stronger. By facing these challenges head-on, you cultivate resilience, developing the ability to bounce back from adversity with newfound determination and resilience.

Consider another example of you deciding to relocate to a foreign land to pursue your ambition, where you do not know their language and are unfamiliar with their customs. Everything you face, such as shopping, transactions, and official work, would be challenging. You will be forced to confront uncertainty and overcome obstacles. While expressing your comfort within yourself, you will be resilient, gradually adapt to the conditions, and perform well. Resilience and adaptability are essential qualities you will eventually gain and create your comfort zone.

Nevertheless, starting something unfamiliar may elicit feelings of apprehension. It is essential to acknowledge that it is a natural part of the growth process and should be embraced as an opportunity for learning and development.

You may say it is easier to say than face in real life. But, if you examine your past life experience, you will notice that you have exercised this many times.

For instance, consider that you have decided to switch careers to pursue your ambition but feel anxious about the uncertainties that lie ahead. Instead of ignoring these feelings, you may recognise them as signs of stepping outside your comfort zone and view them as opportunities for personal growth. By confronting these emotions head-on and developing strategies to manage them effectively, such as seeking support from friends, practising mindfulness techniques or engaging with a coach, you can navigate unfamiliar territory with courage and resilience. Ultimately, by acknowledging and embracing these feelings, you can overcome obstacles and reap the rewards of your ambition, leading to a greater sense of fulfilment and accomplishment in the long run.

Moreover, living a life with your genuine ambition will expand your perspective and enrich your understanding of human life and your merciful creator.

You will realise how the universe will be beside you, supporting you by opening unbelievable opportunities. This is similar to performing well in your organisation.

When you perform sincerely and productively in your job, your colleagues, supervisors, and the whole organisation will support you. You will be given special privileges and will be open to contribute further.

The universe operates with specific natural laws. Every element in this universe, including humans, has a particular role.

When each aspect functions as expected, the whole system will become perfect.

Each component will support the other in harmony. When you embark on your genuine ambition, you will directly witness this fantastic experience.

In conclusion, embarking on the path of setting genuine ambitions and stepping out of your comfort zone is a transformative journey that leads to profound personal development and self-realisation. By embracing new challenges, learning from unfamiliar experiences, and venturing into unknown territory, you open yourself up to boundless opportunities for growth. While this journey may demand courage and perseverance, the rewards of pursuing genuine ambitions are immeasurable. They shape you into a more resilient, adaptable, and confident individual, equipping you with the tools and experiences necessary to navigate life's challenges and pursue your dreams with determination. Furthermore, you will meet your merciful creator as a successful performer and be rewarded immensely hereafter. Ultimately, you unlock the potential to lead a purpose-driven life by daring to pursue meaningful ambitions and embrace the discomfort of growth.

Mahatma Gandhi

Mahatma Gandhi, widely regarded as one of the most influential figures in modern history, provides an inspiring example of someone who discovered meaningful ambition after facing personal and professional challenges. Gandhi initially trained as a lawyer in England and later practised law in South Africa, where he became involved in civil rights activism. Despite achieving success in his legal career, Gandhi was profoundly dissatisfied and yearned for a higher purpose in life. It wasn't until Gandhi returned to India in 1915 that he found his true calling as a leader of the Indian independence movement. Inspired by the teachings of nonviolence and civil disobedience, Gandhi began organising peaceful protests and campaigns against British colonial rule.

Through his unwavering commitment to nonviolent resistance, Gandhi galvanised millions of Indians to join the struggle for independence. He led numerous boycotts, marches, and protests, including the famous Salt March in 1930, which played a pivotal role in India's quest for freedom. Despite facing imprisonment, violence, and personal hardship, Gandhi remained dedicated to his cause, believing in the power of love, truth, and nonviolence to bring about social change.

Gandhi's journey from a disillusioned lawyer to a revered nation leader underscores the transformative power of discovering meaningful ambition. His life is a timeless example of how one person's dedication to a noble cause can inspire movements, change hearts and minds, and ultimately shape history. Gandhi's legacy inspires generations of activists, leaders, and ordinary people to strive for a better world based on truth, justice, and compassion.

REFLECTION

Here are some quizzes designed to assess your understanding of the chapter's content, your critical thinking skills regarding the concepts discussed, and your ability to apply these concepts in real-life situations.

Before proceeding to the next chapter, take some time to review these questions. This will help reinforce the chapter's key points and enable you to develop your insights.

Quiz 1: Comprehension

1. How important is it for you to live a life aligned with your genuine ambition?

   What benefits do you believe you would gain from pursuing your true calling?

2. Consider when you faced uncertainty or challenges in pursuing a goal.

   How did you demonstrate resilience and adaptability in that situation?

   What did you learn from overcoming those obstacles?

3. How do you believe this journey of self-discovery can lead to greater fulfilment and purpose?

Quiz 2: Critical Thinking

1. Consider the examples in the chapter, such as enrolling in an art class or switching careers.

   How do these examples resonate with your experiences or desires for personal growth and exploration?

2. Consider the example of starting a business in an unfamiliar industry or relocating to a foreign country.

   How might you apply the principles of resilience and adaptability to navigate such situations effectively?

3. Reflect on the analogy of performing well in an organisation and receiving support from colleagues and supervisors.

   How might this concept apply to your journey of pursuing genuine ambitions and experiencing support from the universe?

Quiz 3: Application

1. How might you implement strategies such as seeking support from friends or engaging with a coach to navigate unfamiliar territory with courage and resilience?

2. Reflect on your own experiences of stepping outside your comfort zone.

   How did you manage feelings of apprehension or anxiety in those moments?

   What strategies helped you overcome those feelings and move forward?

Consider the long-term rewards of pursuing genuine ambitions in this life and hereafter. How do these potential rewards motivate you to embrace discomfort and pursue meaningful goals?

7

CONCLUSION

We discussed about 'ambition'. Until people discover their genuine ambitions, they will spend their valuable time, effort, and money on various wishful goals based on momentary desires or external factors.

Having ambition is not something optional. According to what we argued in this book, making your world life highly meaningful is a promising aspect.

The notion of the negative impacts of ambition is due to the lack of understanding about what ambition is and how to discover it.

Recognising the potential drawbacks of unchecked ambition can help individuals channel their power in ways aligned with their values and promote overall well-being.

Genuine ambitions should be built upon your innate potential, while wishful ambitions are influenced by external factors such as peers, parents, teachers, colleagues, and community pressure. While you take guidance from external factors, you should depend on your potential to discover your genuine ambitions.

Thus, external factors may help you to know what others see within you, what they expect from you, and what your apparent potential is.

Autonomy and self-awareness are crucial; a reliable and experienced coach can help you significantly.

Discovering your ambition is a transformative experience. You need to do this exercise once in your life.

Hence, you must invest seriously in this process. People spend time and money to get some certificates, but most of the time, those certificates will not benefit them in their careers; they purchase many things that they will use only a few times in their whole life or procure some properties, but they will never benefit from them.

However, people fail to invest in discovering their genuine ambitions, which will promise them a happy life in this world and the hereafter.

We discussed seven simple steps for discovering your ambition. Each step is crucial to ensuring genuine ambition.

It is vital to plan a career that aligns with your ambition. Then, you will enjoy a wonderful life filled with many blessings. However, this is not always a reality.

Most people are working on something they don't want to continue. Hence, balancing your ambition and unaligned career is essential until you find and switch to the right job to help you realise your ambition.

The decision to depart your current career must be made with proper transition planning to minimise potential risks.

Therefore, engaging a reliable mentor or coach is very important to help you move from where you are to where you deserve to be.

The world you are living in is bombarded with tons of information. Because of that, you are confused about 'who are you?' and 'what you can do at your best?'.

Although you were created with a purpose and the ability to live a focused life, you find it comfortable to stay wherever you are.

Therefore, once you discover your ambition, you must make a firm decision, step out of your comfort zone, and start your journey.

Hence, convincing yourself of the promising rewards in this world and hereafter is essential.

Indeed, discovering genuine ambitions is the greatest blessing one could have in this life.

By daring to pursue genuine ambitions and embracing the discomfort accompanying growth, you unlock the potential to lead a more heart-warming and purpose-driven life.

Ultimately, your ambition will make you more resilient, adaptable, and self-assured.

BIBLIOGRAPHY

Altalib, H. (2001). Training guide for Islamic workers (No. 1). International Institute of Islamic Thought (IIIT).

Anderson, A. H. (2000). *Training in Practice: Successful Implementation of Plans*. Infinity Books.

Champy, J., & Nohria, N. (2000). *The Arc of Ambition: Defining the Leadership Journey*. Perseus Books Group.

Coulter, M. K., & Coulter, M. K. (2008). Strategic management in action.

Duckworth, A. (2016). *Grit: The power of passion and perseverance*. Scribner.

Hersey, P., & Blanchard, K. H. (1969). Management of organisational behavior: Utilizing human resources.

Merrill, D. W., & Reid, R. H. (1981). *Personal styles & effective performance*. CRC Press.

Rafiudeen, M. M. (2024). Global Mind Strategic Leader, Amazon.com

Rafiudeen, M. N. (2024). Discover the Leader Within You, Amazon.com

Rafiudeen, M. N., Ramzy, M. I., & Razak, A. Z. B. A. (2023). Talent Scouting: Lessons from Prophet Muhammad, Universiti Malaya Press, Universiti Malaya.

Richards, R. (2020). *Ambition: Why it's good to want more and how to get it*. Penguin Books.

Ulrich, D., & Ulrich, D. (2018). The leadership capital index: Realizing the market value of leadership. Berrett-Koehler Publishers.

AUTHOR

Dr Mohamed Nismy is a human resource development strategist, author, accomplished trainer, leadership coach, and management consultant with over two decades of experience. With a professional foundation as a Civil Engineer, he has spent more than ten years contributing to the Oil and Gas industry, holding key positions such as Quality Assurance Engineer and Strategic Business Planner.

A commitment to excellence marks his academic journey. He holds both B.Sc. and M.Sc. degrees in Engineering, an MBA (UK), and an MA (IOU) in Islamic Studies. He completed his PhD at the University of Malaya on "Identification of Talents for Effective Utilisation of People." Presently, Dr. Mohamed Nismy is an Elite Fellow at UM.

Dr. Mohamed Nismy is a certified life coach, executive coach, leadership coach and an accredited professional advanced trainer (ILM).

The amalgamation of his multi-disciplinary qualifications uniquely positions him to offer transformative training and consulting services to professionals and businesses of diverse backgrounds. Dr Mohamed Nismy's specialisation lies in sustainable Human Resources Development, and his expertise spans Strategic Planning.

His impact extends far and wide. He has positively influenced thousands of individuals through training and coaching programs and conducts corporate training programs covering various topics. Dr. Mohamed Nismy combines academic prowess with practical experience, offering a holistic approach to HR development.

LM GLOBAL CONSULTANCY

Your HR Development Partner

Everyone has unique built-in potential, which could be capitalised on through effective consultation to become a *global mind*.

A Global Mind recognises and utilises their built-in potential to demonstrate extraordinary performance in their profession and achieve a successful life enriched with Universal Values.

At Leaders Mind Global, we employ all the best possible techniques to identify your potential and readiness to facilitate your development roadmap with solid measures. We specialise in providing Training, Coaching, and Management Consultancy services. We empower people and businesses to achieve sustainable development through the optimal use of their innate potential.

We envision a productive work culture where leaders and professionals thrive and are committed to achieving excellence. Our firm belief that "Will to good change is the way to success" motivates us to leave no stone unturned in ensuring the success of our clients.

www.leadersmindglobal.com

www.ingramcontent.com/pod-product-compliance
Lightning Source LLC
LaVergne TN
LVHW091123150826
845673LV00002B/949

* 9 7 9 8 2 3 0 1 6 1 0 3 5 *